BUGS

Words by
Catherine Bailey

Pictures by
Lauren Eldridge

L B

LITTLE, BROWN AND COMPANY

New York Boston

Secret cities buzz and bustle
with itty-bitty hard-work hustle.

Crouch down low.
Hush. You'll see

how bugs build
a community.

Like humans who live and work together in towns and cities, different bugs have unique skills that combine to create a world where everyone—even people— depends on one another.

Ants inside a crumbling tree

chew through wood and clear debris.

Like builders clearing a construction site, **carpenter ants** rebuild our forests by breaking down old timber, which makes room for new plants and trees.

rolling poo (ew!), mixing soil.

Ladybugs on patrol.
Polka-dot pest control.

Like police officers protecting
a neighborhood, **ladybugs**
protect flower and vegetable
gardens from aphids and other
tiny pests.

Grasshoppers chop and chew,
trimming plants like gardeners do.

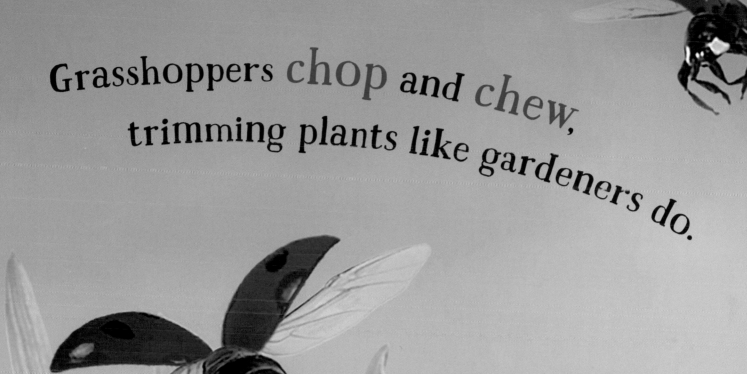

Like landscapers mowing lawns, **grasshoppers** prevent overgrowth by eating through leaves, weeds, and grass.

To save their nest, termites fight.
Mandibles chomp and bite!

Like soldiers who serve and protect, **termites** defend their communities with various weapons, including snapping jaws!

Down underground. Up in trees.
All alone. In colonies.

Digging, dragging, trekking, trapping.
Bugs work hard. Overlapping.

Like residents of any community, some bugs work together while others work alone—but everything a bug does impacts those around it.

Honey hives, like factories,

whir with busy worker bees.

Like manufacturers making products, **honeybees** create honey and beeswax that both humans and animals can use.

Butterflies dance to and fro.
They pollinate and help plants grow.

Like gardeners planting seeds, butterflies spread pollen— which helps plants grow—when they flit and fly from one flower to another.

Rain or shine, sleet or snow, it's one **big bug world** on the go!

Like postal workers who deliver mail in any kind of weather, bugs get their jobs done in every climate.

Spiders plan perfect traps
with lacy nets that won't collapse.

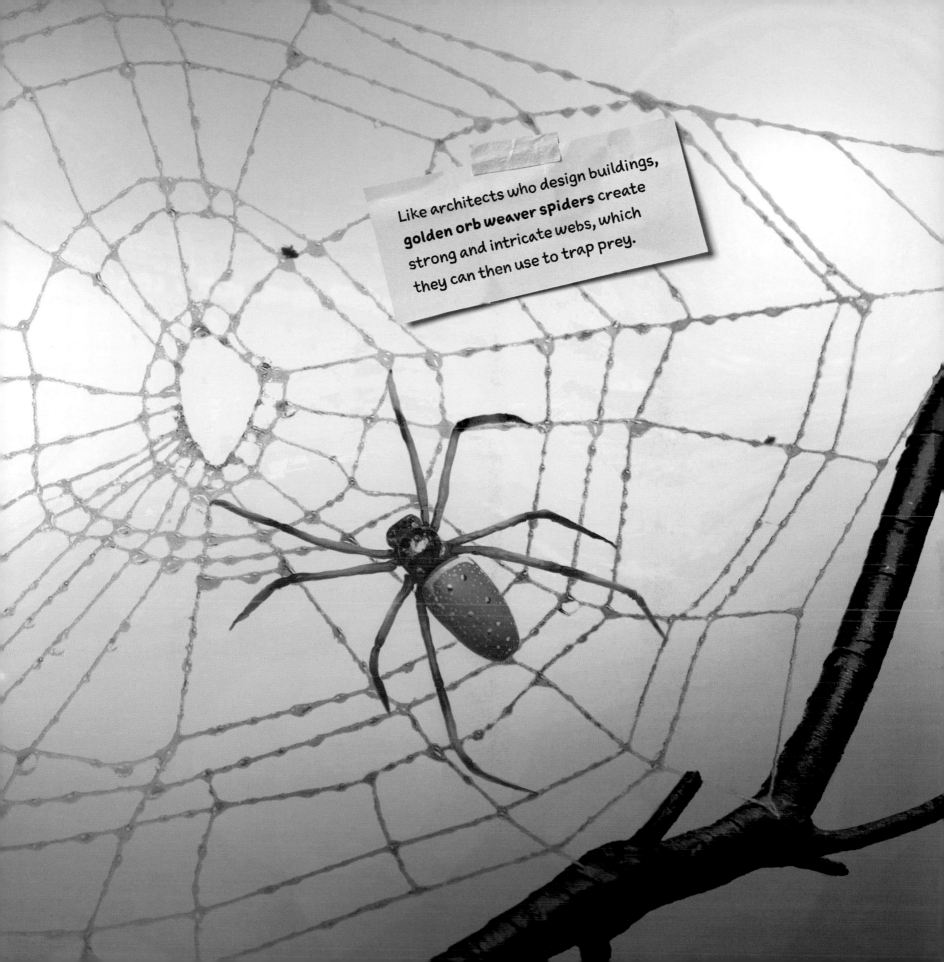

Like architects who design buildings, **golden orb weaver spiders** create strong and intricate webs, which they can then use to trap prey.

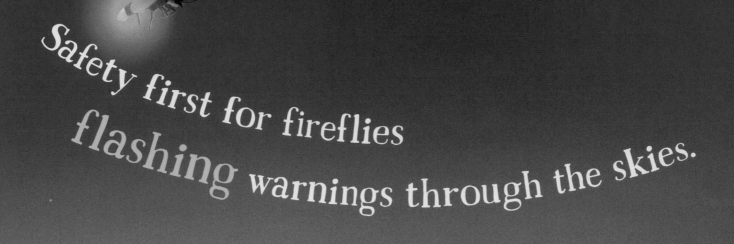

Safety first for fireflies
flashing warnings through the skies.

Like park rangers who protect visitors from wild animals, **fireflies** flash their lights to warn away predators such as bats, birds, and even some lizards.

Spitting, spinning silky threads,
little worms make their beds.

Like weavers spinning yarn, **silkworms** create cocoons of silk that they then sleep in until they become moths.

Crickets croon a twilight tune
with beating wings beneath the moon.

Like musicians making melodies, male **crickets** create distinctive sounds by rubbing their wings together to entertain and attract attention—usually from female crickets.

So if you see rustling leaves
or hear a hum on nighttime's breeze,
remember: busy bugs work day and night,
side by side, in plain sight.

Fun Buggy Facts

Bugs all around you are building their itty-bitty cities *right now*. And whether they work alone or in a team, each one has an important role to play. These busy bugs impact not only *their* community but yours as well. You might know that humans use bug-made products, like honey and silk, but did you know…

- When bugs dig through the dirt, they break up the hard ground and leave behind nutrients so that new plants can grow. These new plants—from fruits and vegetables to trees—provide food, shelter, and oxygen to humans.

- When bugs eat other critters, they get rid of dangerous pests, like mosquitoes. These pests hurt humans by carrying diseases and attacking gardens, farms, and more.

- When a big bug eats a smaller one, the smaller bug provides the big one with fuel and protein. And the big bug might then become a meal for an even bigger animal—which maintains our food chain.

- When bugs travel from one flower to another, they spread pollen, which helps new flowers grow. These flowers can provide medicine, food, and natural dyes—as well as something beautiful to enjoy.

- When bugs chew, chomp, and gnaw through garbage, plants, and trees, they break them down and create nutrients. This recycling of materials keeps our earth clean and healthy.

- When bugs produce their own light, they create chemicals that help scientists with medical research. The process of living creatures like fireflies making light is very rare and is called bioluminescence.

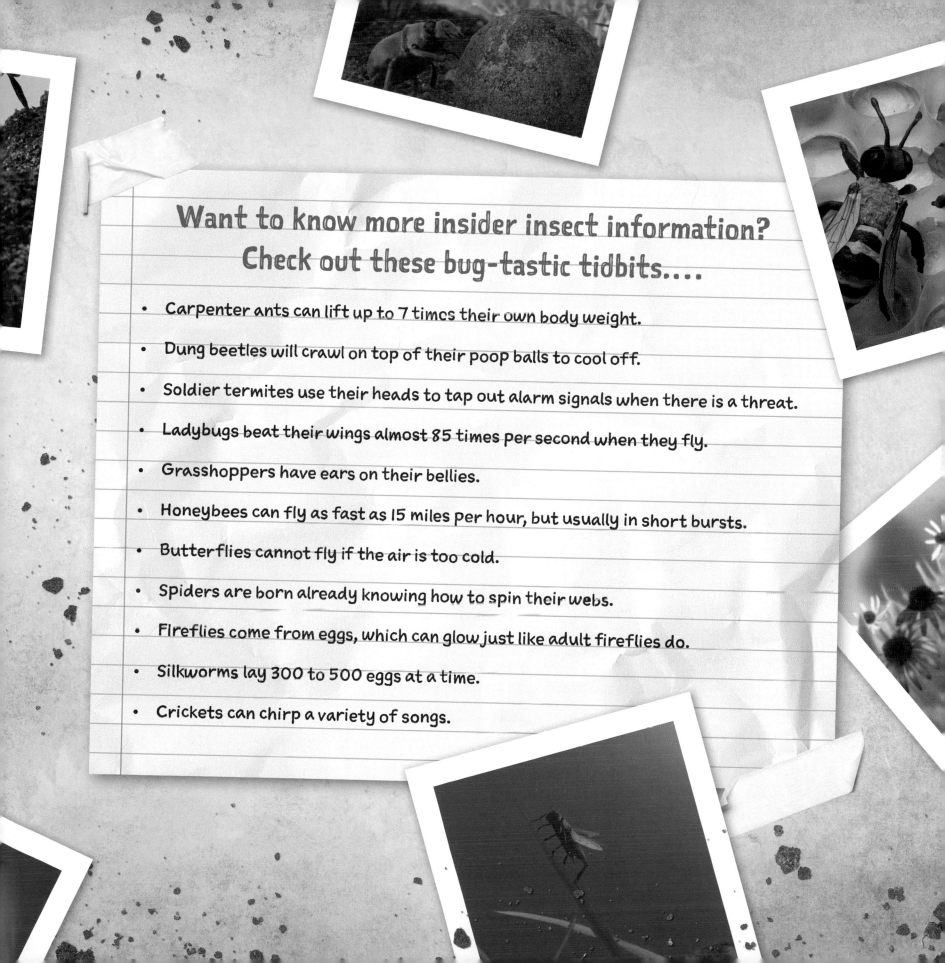

Want to know more insider insect information?
Check out these bug-tastic tidbits....

- Carpenter ants can lift up to 7 times their own body weight.

- Dung beetles will crawl on top of their poop balls to cool off.

- Soldier termites use their heads to tap out alarm signals when there is a threat.

- Ladybugs beat their wings almost 85 times per second when they fly.

- Grasshoppers have ears on their bellies.

- Honeybees can fly as fast as 15 miles per hour, but usually in short bursts.

- Butterflies cannot fly if the air is too cold.

- Spiders are born already knowing how to spin their webs.

- Fireflies come from eggs, which can glow just like adult fireflies do.

- Silkworms lay 300 to 500 eggs at a time.

- Crickets can chirp a variety of songs.

A Note from the Artist

When I first read Catherine Bailey's fantastic text, I knew I wanted to create a vibrant, texture-rich world that would encourage readers to take a closer look. Because *Hustle Bustle Bugs* is all about exploring the environment and noticing busy bugs around us, I decided to incorporate as many natural elements as possible into my artwork, such as dried flower petals, sticks, crushed leaves, and plenty of real dirt and grass.

But wait! Don't artists use pencils and paints to create a book's illustrations? Well, some do, but I use whatever materials work best for the story, building scenes and characters out of everyday objects, craft supplies, and things you might find in your backyard. The bugs themselves are made mainly of wire, epoxy putty, tinfoil, mini foam footballs, polymer clay, vellum, and acrylic paint. The only exceptions are the butterflies—which I created out of yupo paper, alcohol ink, hand-cut black card stock, polymer clay, acrylic paint, and wire—and the silkworms—which are made from hair curlers covered with foam, fabric paint, and painted pinheads. The sisters who explore the busy bug world are made from wire, epoxy putty, polymer clay, acrylic eyes, and acrylic paint. They were inspired by my own two daughters, so I cut and hand-sewed their outfits from pieces of my girls' old clothing.

You might be surprised to learn that the environments in this book are actually *smaller* than the bugs and girls in them. When creating each illustration, I lit and photographed the setting first, then took pictures of the individual characters. This let me put several photos together like pieces of a puzzle to make the final scene. There's no one way to illustrate a book, and I hope learning about how the art in this one was made (and about the amazing, bustling bugs right outside your door) will make you want to create something new and explore your world!

—Lauren Eldridge

For my mom, Sally, who taught me to hustle,
make nests, and love books —CB

To Luca, Elsa, and all the Larrys they've cared
for throughout the years —LE

About This Book

The photographs for this book were taken using a Nikon D7200 with a 35mm lens, and the images were composited digitally. This book was edited by Deirdre Jones and designed by Neil Swaab. The production was supervised by Patricia Alvarado, and the production editor was Marisa Finkelstein. The text was set in Mrs Ant and Sketchnote Text, and the display type is Sketchnote Square.

Little, Brown and Company
Hachette Book Group
1290 Avenue of the Americas, New York, NY 10104
Visit us at LBYR.com

First Edition: February 2022

Little, Brown and Company is a division of Hachette Book Group, Inc.
The Little, Brown name and logo are trademarks of Hachette Book Group, Inc.

The publisher is not responsible for websites (or their content) that are not owned by the publisher.

Image credits: The first page of text is page 1. Various vintage notepapers on jacket and pages 3, 6, 7, 11, 15, 16, 17, 19, 23, 25, and 31 copyright © Picsfive/Shutterstock.com; various real brown paper torn or ripped pieces of paper on jacket and pages 5, 13, and 21 copyright © Fierman Much/Shutterstock.com; white notepaper on page 30 copyright © ESB Professional/Shutterstock.com; images of adhesive tape on pages 5, 13, 21, 28, 29, 30, and 31 copyright © Picsfive/Shutterstock.com; images of dirt on pages 28, 29, 30, and 31 copyright © xpixel/Shutterstock.com; vintage old paper texture on pages 28, 29, 30, and 31 copyright © Horenk0/Shutterstock.com; crumped paper texture on page 28 copyright © NOK FreeLance/Shutterstock.com; lined paper background on page 29 copyright © The_Pixel/Shutterstock.com.

Library of Congress Cataloging-in-Publication Data
Names: Bailey, Catherine (Children's story writer), author. | Eldridge, Lauren, illustrator.
Title: Hustle bustle bugs / words by Catherine Bailey; pictures by Lauren Eldridge.
Description: New York : Little, Brown and Company, 2022. | Audience: Ages 4–8. | Summary: "Bugs, including ants, beetles, grasshoppers, and more, have unique skills that combine to create a world where everyone—even people—depends on one another. "—Provided by publisher.
Identifiers: LCCN 2020048428 | ISBN 9780759557406 (hardcover)
Subjects: LCSH: Insects—Juvenile literature. | Insects—Behavior—Juvenile literature.
Classification: LCC QL467.2 .B353 2022 | DDC 595.7—dc23
LC record available at https://lccn.loc.gov/2020048428

ISBN 978-0-7595-5740-6

PRINTED IN CHINA

APS

10 9 8 7 6 5 4 3 2 1